This book is given with love:

_____

_____

ISBN: 978-1-949474-20-6

Edition: September 2019

For all inquiries, please contact us at:

info@puppysmiles.org

To see more of our books, visit us at:

www.PuppyDogsAndIceCream.com

BIRDS, BEASTS, CRITTERS & CREATURES:
THE STORY OF NOAH'S ARK

BY: JIMMY LYNN   ILLUSTRATED BY: ANA NGUYEN

The largest thunderstorm, the world had ever seen...
covered God's great Earth, all things growing and green.

Washing the land, of all that's not good,
He chose a man named Noah to build an Ark of wood.

With the boat near completion,
and only seven days to spare.

Noah beckoned all animals,
every boy and girl pair.

At first came the birds,
by waddle and by flight.
Then reptiles and mammals,
loading day and night.

11

Another clap of thunder,
as the water began to rise.
Crisp bolts of lightning,
as the waves grew in size.

Spooky nocturnal creatures,
who only come out at night.

Scorpions, bats, and even the spiders,
Noah made sure they're alright.

15

Tigers don't like baths,
and cheetahs can't stand the rain.

16

After 40 stormy nights,
the kitty-cats went insane.

17

At the back of the boat,
with strong winds and a howl...

The dogs all greet Noah,
big wags and no growl.

19

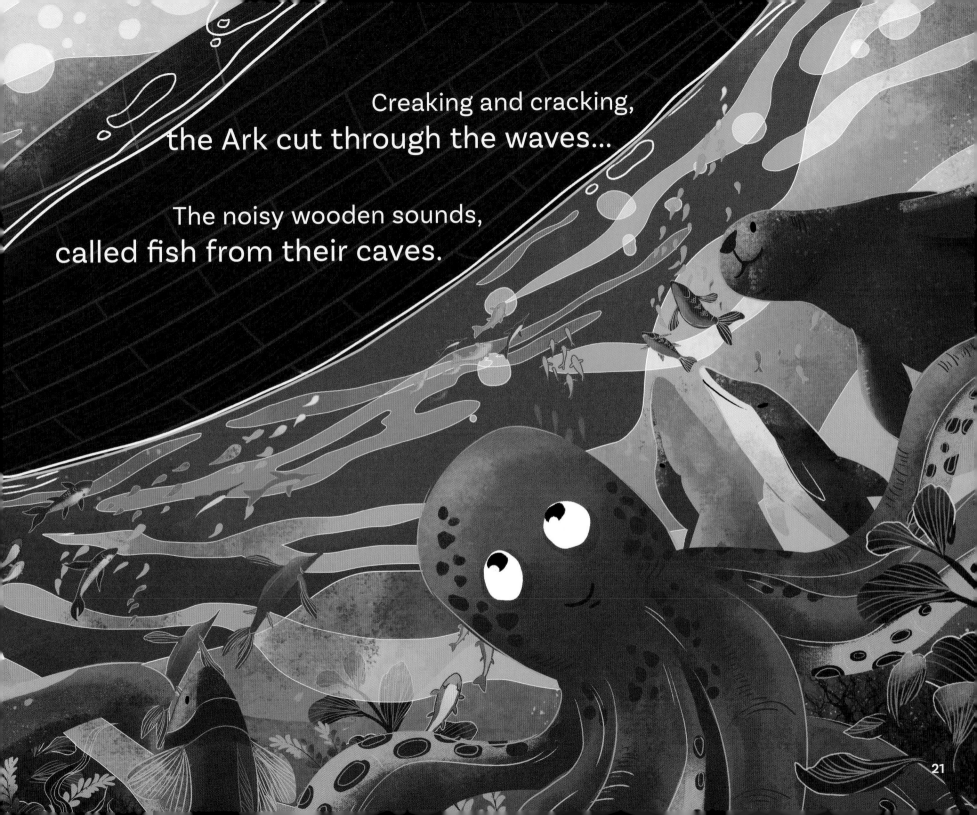

Creaking and cracking,
the Ark cut through the waves...

The noisy wooden sounds,
called fish from their caves.

In the belly of the great Ark,
where giraffes and zebras hung-out.

Packed together so tightly...
they could hardly move about!

24

But the noisiest pairs,
came from birds of a feather,
With toucans and peacocks,
they all squawked together.

Cold-blooded creatures
need warmth to be strong.
Noah promised them sunshine,
soon the clouds would be gone.

As the downpour continued,
and the hard winds did blow...

A glimmer of sunshine,
slowly warmed the rhino.

29

The polar bears welcomed Noah,
with his red cheeks aglow...

The best place on the Ark,
is where penguins dance in the snow.

30

With creepy crawly features,
bugs can be scary and gross.

But most are quite beautiful,
just take time to look close.

Monkeys are mischievous,
like kids on a sugar-kick.

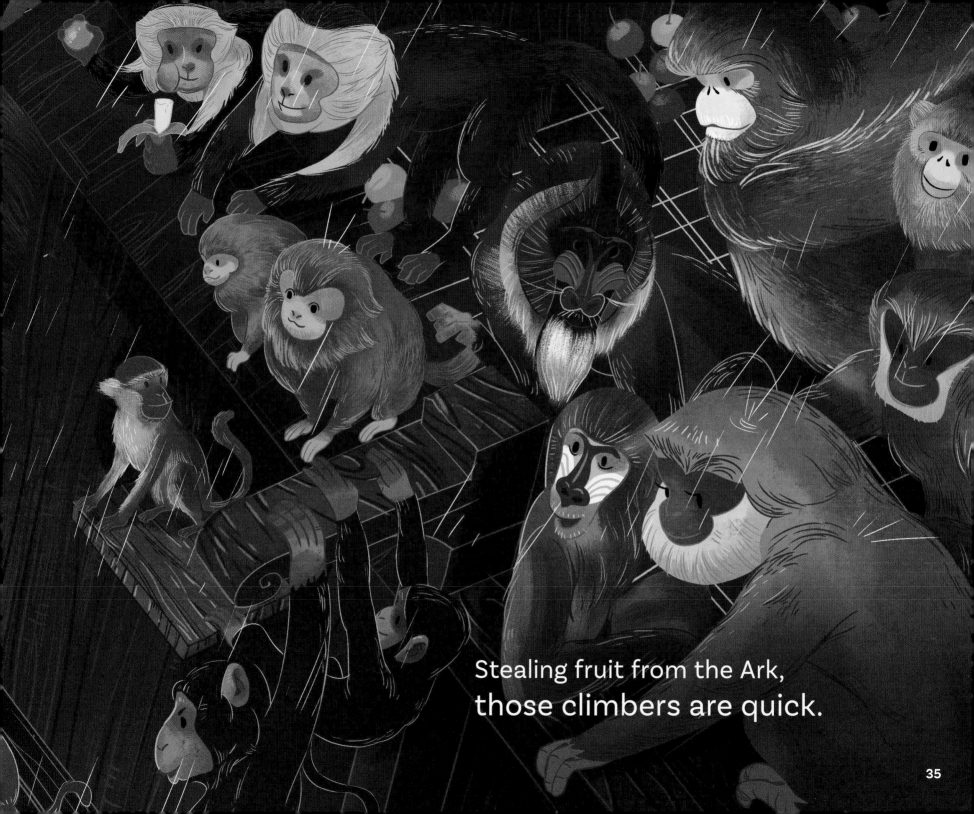

Stealing fruit from the Ark,
those climbers are quick.

35

As the sun shined upon the water,
the Ark sped toward dry land.

All of the animals had made it,
and would soon touch the sand.

37

After 40 days of adventure,
and 40 moons of goodnight,
Life would begin again,
a fresh rainbow and sunlight.

🐾 Claim Your FREE Gift!

Visit ➡ 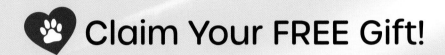 PDICBooks.com/noah

Thank you for purchasing Birds, Beasts, Critters & Creatures, and welcome to the Puppy Dogs & Ice Cream family.

We're certain you're going to love the little gift we've prepared for you at the website above.